Echoes of Victorian Poetry in Selected Works of Robert Browning

Echoes of Victorian Poetry in Selected Works of Robert Browning

Ritu Pandey

Published in 2024 by Notionpress, India

E-mail: ritu@uniteduniversity.edu.in

Echoes of Victorian Poetry in Selected Works of Robert Browning

Copyright © Dr. Ritu Pandey

ISBN : 979886320364

Content

About the Author

Dr. Ritu Pandey is a recipient of Mahatma Jyotiba Phule Fellowship National Award 2022 and Author of the book, *The World Of Charles Dickens*. She is currently teaching as Assistant Professor (English Literature and Language) at United University and resides in Prayagraj, India.

With an experience span of 12 years, she has taught in various reputed institutes of her city; Mahila Sewa Sadan, Ewing Christian College, CMP Degree College and Allahabad Degree College.

She obtained her D.Phil degree from University of Allahabad on the topic *"The Child Characters in the Novels of Charles Dicken : A Critical Study.*

Foreword

The book "Echoes of Victorian Poetry in Selected works of Robert Browning" written by Dr. Ritu Pandey very metaphorically defines some of the works of Robert Browning, that shows his poetic powers and his maturity in intellectual love of art, religion, men and women invested with color, music and romance. Her book presents a memorable character analysis of different poems, full of incisive and acute insight.

Browning was primarily a poet of man. Thus, he declared that his "stress lay on incidents in the development of the soul." He was a poet of personality and the soul. Men's thoughts, feelings and desires remained his supreme interest from first to the last. But the soul has numerous points of contact with the outer world. These points of contact are Nature, Art, Love, Philosophical belief and Psychology. The book has shown the Alien vision of Victorian Poetry by contrasting the works of the three vital poets of the Victorian Age, Tennyson, Browning and Arnold. Tennyson was the representative poet of his age and was regarded as a Poet Laureate in 1850. Arnold was a melancholic poet whose endeavors were accepted more as a prose writer and a critic. Hugh Walker had rightly stated that Browning was at once astonishingly great and astonishingly faulty. Originality of Browning led him into irritating eccentricities but his reputation by the end of the nineteenth century was at its pinnacle.

The Victorians were seized by doubt and disbelief in faith and religion due to the coming of science and industrialization. They resolved this problem by adopting a middle path of compromise. In her first chapter, "Sense of Fragmentation and the Victorian Age" she delicately talks about the theme of love. Though Tennyson abhorred physical passion, domesticity for him was an obsession, not an ideal. Browning believed that human love is a stepping stone to Divine Love. Optimistic hope governs even failure in love, for life to Browning was a series of existences in different worlds and human efforts are bound to succeed ultimately.

Ritu Pandey has categorically talked about the changes in social order brought about by the change in Politics. Democracy and Liberalization came to the forefront and awakened social consciousness and a humanitarian spirit. They were in a dilemma about religious skepticism. The position of Victorians was of total alienation and consequently more poignant. Arnold believed in fragmentation but Browning strove to reach a "wholeness" through his optimism. The philosophy of Browning is the philosophy of a man looking at the world with more than a glimmer of hope in his eyes. His dramatic Monologues are supposed to be essentially utterances of fictitious figures.

Her second chapter, "Poems of Failure and the Vision of Evil" attempts to bring out a demarcation between Browning's poems that deal with "life affirmation" and those that deal with reverse, namely "life negation". She has brought out the grotesque features in the poems, "Sibrandus Schafnaburgensis", "Holy Cross Day" and "A Toccato at Galuppis's". Browning's vision of evil is seen in his poem, "Rabbi Ben Ezra". His personal cravings are revealed in his monologue "Andrea del Sarto", which clearly states that perfection lies in the aspiration and not in the ultimate achievement. He contrasts this poem with another monologue "Fra Lippo Lippi" in which the priest's admission of truth can be considered a blasphemy by the church authorities, yet Browning believed that ultimately good conquers over evil. "The Last Ride Together" is one of the masterpieces of Browning's monologues. Riding becomes an imaginative stimulus to Browning and live ruptures are self-sufficient and enduring. "Abt Vogler" depicts a musician who believes that the duty of mankind lies in composing beautiful Hymns in praise of God. Throughout life Browning continued his search for originality. He was concerned with men, not mankind. His abiding faith in the essential goodness of man and his saving grace of optimism made him a great poet.

"Childe Roland to the Dark Tower Come" and "Caliban upon Setebos", portrays the child as not a figure of despair, but a figure of valor. He is able to preserve his equilibrium even in the face of despair and horrible sights. "Caliban upon Setebos" is a satire on the anthropomorphic concept of religion.

The last chapter gives a critical analysis of the poem, "La Saisiaz" which clearly states that fancy does not mean poetic imagination but the popular significance of the word named "fiction". Browning's philosophy is very wide. It covers the time past, the time present, and the time future. Having read the poems of Browning, one finds oneself wiser, because his poems are a study in two worlds. Browning's optimism was partly a result of experience-his own joyful personal life and zest for life. Optimism is based on life's realities. Thus the book introspects and reveals that life is full of imperfections but in this very imperfection lies hope, a hope that takes us beyond the portals of death, and it is like a bugle call to good living.

Dr. Neerja Sachdev

Retired Associate Professor

S. S. Khanna Girl's Degree

College, Prayagraj

Preface

The Victorian Age, which was marred by pessimism, and which was disrupted by the forces of disintegration was best represented in the works of Tennyson and Arnold. Robert Browning unlike his contemporaries has often been accrued of glib optimism. The problem of the age was to reconcile faith with science. The Victorians were caught up in a maze, the two opposing forces were (1) the intellect denying a God, and (2) a faith hankering after some Divine Power. With Browning:

"God's in his heaven

All's right with the world."

Like a typical Victorian, he worked for a compromise. His faith and hope which remained unshaken to the end were not achieved without trial, doubt and self – examination.

In this book I have endeavored to do an insightful study of Browning's works, which have expressed his philosophical beliefs. He was primarily a poet of man. There isn't any doubt that the best works of Browning are those in which the poet is most heavily disguised for whereas the subjective poet is basically a lyric poet, whose imagination flights are sustained by the intensity of his personal vision, the objective poet is basically a detached observer of life in all its complexity of forms.

Browning strove to reach a unity of vision and salvage some of the faith that was slowly slipping away from the Victorian world. In order to express his ideas, he chose a suitable medium, the dramatic lyrics. He used a wide variety of ideas and forms.

The form of poetry which inevitably goes together with Robert Browning's Dramatic Monologue. He has been universally acclaimed for mastering the form. The Dramatic Monologues of Browning do not merely embody a mood rather they evoke an atmosphere of their own. The form was not only utilized by Browning for bringing out human follies and flaws but was used by him for presenting an elaborate argument to prove his beliefs.

One aspect of Browning's poetry is the portrayal of love between man and woman. The love can be like the passion of Ottima in '*Pippa Passes*' in contrast to the romantic love as represented in '*The Last Ride Together*'. In the later poem he maturely handles the rejection of the lover at the hands of his mistress. The dejected lover blesses his mistress and wishes his love to be accomplished in Heaven.

Chapter I

Sense of Fragmentation and the Victorian Age

"The important writing of the Victorian period is to a large extent the product of a double awareness. This was a literature addressed . . . . to the particular temper of mind which had grown up within a society seeking adjustment to the conditions of modern life."[1]

"Thus it came about that the double awareness which so generally characterized the Victorian literary mind, grew almost into a perpetual state of consciousness in three poets through their efforts to work out a new aesthetic position for the artist."[2]

The position of Tennyson, Browning and Arnold, lies between the Romantics and Pre-Raphaelites. Of the three, Tennyson succeeded in conforming to the Victorian ideas and

---

[1]   The Alien Vision of Victorian Poetry. E.D.H. Johnson (ix). New Jersey, 1952.
[2]   Ibid. (xiii) New Jersey, 1952.

was consequently accepted by the public. He received wide adulation and was declared Poet Laureate in 1850. Arnold's poetic endeavors were accepted only after he had turned to *prose*. Browning's progress was more gradual. Perhaps there is no nineteenth century poet whose ultimate position in the hierarchy is as doubtful as that of Browning. He is at once, astonishingly great - and faulty. He has original ideas, but his eccentricities appear to outnumber them, yet his works are remarkably independent. There is no element of revolt, which underlies much of Tennyson's works.

Browning remains uniform and contrasts with his contemporaries in his remarkable independence. He is self-sustained and his method of conception is his own. Despite their individual characteristics, the literary works of Tennyson, Browning and Arnold present a number of striking parallels. Their earlier works are pre-eminently introspective and at places didactic in tone. This cloistral element is gradually replaced by the awareness of contemporary events and mood. The optimum of the nineteenth century was not a very spontaneous quality. The Victorians lived, as *John Drinkwater* said: "in an atmosphere of violent uncertainty." They thus turned to subconscious suggestions. They however, could not escape from three unpleasant truths - democracy, growth of disbelief and sex. They approached these problems from a gentle angle of compromise.

Of these three compromises, the one that covered sex problem was the most blatant, and persistent - and successful. Their object was to discover some middle course between unbridled licentiousness - and complete negation of the functions and purposes of nature. The Victorians believed that the British race should be propagated, and decided that this biological necessity could be elevated into a moral - nay even a civic virtue. In this way evolved the ideal of the English home.

Tennyson was singularly well-adapted to the reception and exploitation of this ideal. His treatment of the theme of love was not only manly, but wholesome. Apart from the control over, or abhorrence of physical passion, Tennyson possessed an almost feminine sympathy for the tender delicacies of the home. Domesticity was for Tennyson, not so much an ideal, as an obsession.

This abhorrence of "illicit" relations was not present in Robert Browning. In him, the intellectual element was too powerful to allow predominance of sensuousness, even when the poet is dealing with relations of the sexes. Secondly, Browning's poems and monologues are utterances of fruition, the person looks to the present and the past - as well as to the future. Browning's works are mainly dramatic and contain a peculiar charm. The passion of love is *individualized* in the works of Browning.

The second problem present in the Victorian Age, dealt with politics. Changes took place in England between the early thirties, and 1886. During the years the English body politic had passed from the phase of aristocratic Whiggism, through middle-class Liberalism, to the achievements of democracy as is enjoyed today. The age was one of ferment. Among the seeming vortex of ideas there were two main currents, Democracy, and Science.

The political unrest, combined with the misery that followed the Industrial Revolution, awakened social consciousness, and a humanitarian spirit. During this time, England made enormous material progress; and contemporary literature tended to excessive materialism in thought. The Romantic Age was so concerned with adventure, romance, revolution and the ideals of equality, liberty and fraternity. The Victorians had been badly jolted by the new findings of science, and consequently did not want further excitement. They wished to be soothed and assured. The *National Review* explained the prevailing mood thus: "we ask for rest; for passionless calm, and silence unproved."[3]

The Victorians valued the external accuracy of presentation and cared little for personal truth and emotion. In the works of art they preferred the element of recognition to that of imagination. The poets were products of their environment.

The final problem prevalent in C 19th was the general diffusion of religious skepticism. Frightened and appalled by Darwinian conclusions regarding the origin of man and the earth, the Victorians desired to be soothed, and assured that all was for the best. They looked for some compromise between actual knowledge and their blind faith in the ultimate purpose behind the universe.

---

[3]   "The Victorian Age" - Rai Yami.

This then, was the mission of the poets, particularly Arnold and Tennyson. The compromise that they evolved served their generation as a courageous answer to the moral uncertainties of the day.

The problem was to reconcile faith with science. The Victorians were caught up in a maze, the two opposing forces were (1) the intellect denying a God, and (2) a faith hankering after some Divine Power. Arnold's melancholy was the typical outcome of his place in history and his intellect. He felt that there could be no material cure. Neither could he assert, with Browning -

> "God's in his heaven
>
> All's right with the world."[4]

Like a typical Victorian, he worked for a compromise. He felt that reason and test for experience had made belief in the

---

[4]   Pippa Passes, Lines, published.

supernatural impossible. With "Literature and Dogma"[5], he broke off with all orthodox Christianity, and rejected all miracles, including 'Incarnation'. He thus had no creed, only boundless sympathy.

The position of the Victorian poet was thus that of an alien-indecisive. He could neither identify himself with his public, nor reach peace of mind through self-identification. The Romantic bard too was an alien. But his position was more assured due to his sense of completeness . . . . his estrangement from the public did not degenerate to self-alienation.

This ray of faith had made the words of the Romantics prophetic. Their balanced personality is reflected in their poems. Contrary to the fore mentioned, the position of the Victorians, (particularly poets) was of total alienation, and

---

[5]   'Literature and Dogma', M. Arnold, published 1873.

consequently more poignant. In a letter addressed to his sister, Arnold said:

"My poems are fragments . . . that is I am fragments"

This frame of mind was a result of the disintegrating ethos of the time, in which the Victorian bard lived and composed. The poets failed to reach a wholeness of vision . . . a totality in their lives, and this introduced the note of doubt in their poetry. As E.D.H. Johnson writes:, "The reader who comes to the Victorians without bias must be struck again and again by the under-lying tone of unrest. . . ."[6]

The forces of disintegration that tended to disrupt the calmness of the Victorian Age, were felt by Browning, as intensely as by his competitors. The difference was that he was confident in an age when many were unsure. He was perfectly aware of the evil that existed, but he was equally certain of

---

[6]   The Alien Vision of Victorian Poetry. E.D.H. Johnson (ix) New Jersey, 1952.

achieving good through the trial of suffering. Alienation had an effect on Browning's poetry, though he does not express it directly. It is an oblique presence. Tennyson and Arnold expressed it directly, but in the works of Browning its presence below the surface of his optimism - deepens his optimism.

Browning has been accused of *glib* optimism. Eliot feels that his knowledge of the human heart is "adulterated by an optimism, which has proved offensive to our times. "But to accuse Browning of glib philosophy is to read him superficially. Few poets have a deeper understanding of human frailty and failure than Browning. His faith and hope which remained unshaken to the end, were not achieved without trial, doubt and self-examination. He strove to reach a "wholeness", an integration - to check the feeling of his faith slowly crumbling and dwindling into dust. This search for a totality - for the "white-light" as Browning referred to it, is seen in all his major works, as well as in his letters. He writes to Elizabeth Barrett

Barrett:

> "You speak out *you* - I only make men and
>
> women speak - give you truth broken into
>
> prismatic hues, and fear of pure white light. . . ."[7]

Earlier, I had referred to two groups of pets. The former are alien to their contemporaries, but their position as prophet is nevertheless assured. The tone in their works does not lose its poise.

"A divorce between the artist and society first became conspicuous as an element of the Romantic Movement, but even though they had to endure abuse or neglect, the Romantics did not in any case think of themselves as abdicating the poet's traditional right to speak for his age. Blake, Coleridge, Words-worth, Byron, Shelley, Keats were all, it is true, keenly

---

[7]   Letter from R.B. to E.B.B. Hatcham, Surrey, Jan 13, 1845.

sensitive to their generation's reluctance to pay attention to what they were saying, but they accepted isolation as a necessary consequence of their revolutionary progress."[8]

The position of the second group of poets is more poignant. They not only feel cut off from social moods and norms, but are *Self-alienated.* The result is a search for identity. . . ."As a result, there is recognizable in their work a kind of tension originating in the serious writer's traditional desire to communicate, but to do so without betraying the purity of his creative motive even in the face of a public little disposed to undergo the rigors of aesthetic experience."[9]

The absence of this personal identity is reflected in the disintegrated form of poetry.

---

[8]   The Alien Vision of Victorian Poetry - E.D.H. Johnson (xi, xiii), New Jersey, 1952.

[9]   Ibid.

Throughout Browning's poetic career, we sense him attempting to move towards the synthetic vision of the poets of white-light, and being unable to reach it, due to the disintegrating ethos. His inner conflict gives the poems whatever emotional tension they might have had.

In his earlier poetic career, Browning was influenced by the subjectivism of Shelley. After he wrote "Pauline", he suffered feelings of intense guilt at having presented himself to his audience so nakedly. He then abandoned the direct confessional type of poem, and adopted the mask of impersonality. The unique ideal, Browning felt, would be a poet who combined both subjective and objective genius. They may have been his secret ambition, and this inference is justified from his letter to E.B. Barrett.

". . .what I have printed gives no knowledge of me - it evidences abilities of various kinds, if you will - and a dramatic

sympathy with certain modifications of passion . . . *that* I think -
But I never have begun, even, what I hope I was born to begin
and end - 'R.B. a poem'[10] In an earlier letter, E.B. Barrett had
congratulated Browning for his dual vision. She felt that he had
in his vision two worlds.

"You have in your vision two worlds . . . you are both
subjective and objective in the habits of your mind. You can
deal both with abstract thought and with human passion in the
most passionate sense. Thus, you have an immense grasp in Art;
. . ."[11]

However, Browning's opinion regarding his personal
merits was different. He felt that he had failed as a poet. The
Victorian poets were unsure of themselves. The lyrical form, on
the other hand, is possible only when the poet is confident of his

---

[10]   R.B. to E.B.B. Hatcham (Tuesday, Feb. 11, 1845).
[11]   E.B.B. to R.B. Wimpole Street (Jan. 15, 1845).

message. Poetry thus acquires 'unity' from a "vision", which can be found in the works of Milton and Wordsworth.

In the technical sense, lyrical poetry implies a form of words written to be sung to the lyre or other accompaniment. In its applied or extended meaning it is interpreted as the poetry of personal experience or emotion. In the past, this medium gave the poems their balance and poise. Milton, the Restoration era poet, derived his equanimity from the Christian theology, while Wordsworth, the lake district bard, was a nature mystic. His 'Prelude' is a magnificent saga celebrating the innocence of childhood, and the beneficial influence of nature upon these formative years. The poet sees the whole cosmos in one unified term - Nature! She is at once our mother and our guide. This abiding faith enabled Wordsworth to reach a visionary wholeness, which in turn gave unity to his work.

Due to the constant changes prevalent in the Victorian Age, there was a gradual disintegration of faith. The earlier beliefs in the goodness of man and the Maker had been changed due to the new discoveries in the field of science and astronomy. This social upheaval introduced skepticism, alienation and the first seeds of doubt in the Goodness of the Creator. Consequently, the reader as well as the poet suffered. The absence of personal identity resulted in ennui, which broke the bond between the Victorian poet and his audience. Arnold represents thus, the decline of lyric poetry into the elegiac vein.

It cannot be denied, however, that Browning appeared best when he was most disguised, yet there was a dichotomy between the Poet Browning, and R.B.- the man. The dramatic monologues provided Browning the masks from behind which he spoke. In an age when pronouncement of personal faith became difficult, these individual statements represent experiences of universal significance.

Santayana writes "Our poets are things of shreds and patches; they give us episodes and studies, a sketch of this curiosity, a glimpse of that romance; they have no total vision, no grasp of the whole reality, and consequently no capacity for a sane and steady idealization.

Browning attempted to reach spiritual unity variously. It would be interesting to study his attitudes to Art, Love, Live and God in this light and watch their interconnection.

'The Ring and the Book' is a grand attempt at synthesis. Here a situation is viewed from ten different points of view. All truth is a matter of perspective. Truth is related to events in the same way as point of view is related to landscape. It would be interesting to study this evolution in Browning - that of trying to achieve a presentation of truth, in all its complex totality.

****

Chapter II

Robert Browning : Poems of Failure & *The Vision of Evil*

Browning began his career as a subjective poet. He was influenced by the subjectivism of Shelley, but after he wrote *Pauline,* he suffered feelings of intense guilt, at having presented himself so openly before the public. He could not bear his readers looking too deeply into his personality. He felt that "'the unique ideal would be ... a poet who combined both subjective and objective genius....' If the two faculties were to be combined in the same poet, then the poet would be in the unique position of being able to 'speak out', and achieve Shelleyan abatements of Universal significance, while remaining also in successive poems, the objective poet. This may well have been Browning's ambition, but it remains true that he finds complete expression only when he also achieves complete anonymity...."[12]

There is no doubt that the best works of Browning are those in which the poet is most heavily disguised, for whereas the subjective poet is basically a lyric poet, whose imaginative flights are sustained by the intensity of his personal vision, the objective poet is basically a detached observer of life in all its complexity of forms. He regards himself as a craftsman, aware of his individual talent, but conscious always of the tradition and of his responsibility to his medium. Browning strove to reach a unity of vision and salvage some of the faith that was slowly slipping away from the Victorian world. In order to express his ideas he chose a suitable medium, the dramatic lyrics. These were narrative poems dealing with incidents of some importance and interest. Yet Browning could

---

[12]   "Robert Browning and the Dramatic Monologue: The Impersonal Art" A.R. Jones. pg. 311.

not gain satisfaction and tried to perfect his art by adopting the method of mask or "dramatic monologue". The latter was more complex is nature — here incidents described have shifted from the periphery of the mind (external significance) to enter the world of the inner regions of consciousness (internal significance). *W.B. Yeats* commented on the importance to the post of creating masks when he stated that " ... all happiness depends on the energy to assume the mask of some other self;. We put on a grotesque or solemn painted face to hide us from the terrors of judgment..., one loses the infinite pain of self-realization"[13]

In a sense, dramatic monologue brings out the presentation of a situation more accurately and graphically because it is three dimensional, whereas the narrative poem is two dimensional. In this, Browning established a new relationship between (the)

---

[13]   "Robert Browning and the Dramatic Monologue: The Impersonal Art"
A.R. Jones. pg. 327.

reader and the subject, "the subject.... (is) judged by the reader particularly when the reader subject reveals his weaknesses so blatantly. Browning compels his readers to strike a moral attitude in so far as they are being asked to judge..."[14]   His works can be broadly divided into two categories: those poems that deal with 'life affirmation', and those that deal with the reverse, namely 'life-negation'.

Browning used a wide variety of ideas and forms. Nor did he ignore the shabbier and meaner aspects of nature. He believed that ruggedness is as essential a work of art, as gloominess or extravagance. The fantastic, lopsided and nonsensical are conceived to be the work of man, but this instinct of caricature comes from Nature, which is all full of queer creatures as is the 'sketchbook of Callot'. The supreme use of the grotesque is seen in "Sibrandus Schafnaburgensis",

---

[14]   "Robert Browning and the Dramatic Monologue : The Impersonal Art", A.R. Jones. pg. 328.

"Holy-Cross Day", and "A Toccata at Galuppi's". Here he makes the world stand on its head. Browning never ceased from his fierce hunt for poetic novelty, that is, he never became a conservative. His poems of life-affirmation sing the song of refusal.

The Vision of Evil : Despite his affirmation in the goodness of mankind, and faith in the Divinity of God, Browning was aware of the vision of evil. Flesh and soul, youth and old-age, are dichotomies, and unless these conflicting forces can be resolved, self-awareness is impossible. In this context, we can make a study of "Rabbi Ben Ezra". Browning was not bound by any dogma; his ____ Pop is as free as the Rabbi, but he does deal with the evil predominant in man. These imperfections are but natural and Browning's deep understanding of human frailty and failure prevent him from being unduly harsh and critical. The human follies provoke his amusement, but does not embitter him. The greatest truths can be found side by side, the knaves and rogues of Browning' have a uniform tendency to theism _______ degraded, mean and unsuccessful they may be, yet they claim an awful "alliance with divinity".

However, as we go through the major works of Browning, we realize that this desire (of the poet) to achieve wholeness did not meet with success initially. The personal cravings of Browning are revealed in his monologue "*Andrea del Sarto*". Ironically, the subtitle of this poem is "The Faultless Painter". The irony lies in the fact that although the speaker is a successful painter and craftsman in the eyes of the world, he knows that he has actually failed. According to Andrea, perfection lies in the aspiration, and not in the ultimate achievement. To quote his words:

"A man's reach should exceed his grasp,

Or what's a Heaven for?"

Directly after saying this, Andrea adds:

"........ all his silver grey

Placid and perfect with my art, the worse."

Commenting on the aforementioned monologue, George Santayana writes that "no one who has not known the ashen coldness of despair, could write such a poem. He finds a parallel between Browning, the Victorian Poet, and the protagonist painter. Like Andrea, Browning achieved a totality in poetry, _____ in the sphere of art, but he failed to reach it in his personal life. Thus arose the sense of unfulfillment and regret. Santayana says: "Our poets are things of shreds and patches; they give us episodes and studies, a sketch of this curiosity, a glimpse of that romance, they have no totality of vision, no grasp of the whole reality, and consequently no capacity for a same and steady idealization."[15]

---

[15]   "The Barbaric Genius" George Santayana.

By contrast to the other poems, *Andrea del Sarto* is a study of failure. As dark as the poem is, it is not a tragedy, and it would be untrue to say that the protagonist comes to self-realization and self-knowledge as the monologue progresses.... Andrea is one of the most passive of Browning's speakers, and throughout we notice the simplicity of diction and the occurrence of an unusual number of monosyllabic lines. We can compare and contrast *Andrea del Sarto* with yet another monologue of Browning, titled "Fra Lippo Lippi". Whereas *Fra Lippo* ends with the dawn breaking, *Andrea* is a twilight piece. The tone of "Andrea del Sarto" is correspondingly muted. The source is Vasari's 'Life of Andrea del Sarto'. Obligated to choose perfection of the life or of the work, Andrea has chosen the latter, only to realize that his life is deeply unhappy while his work is too perfect, __________ cripplingly perfect. Painter-like, Browning's creation (the protagonist Andrea) lives in the eye, and it is the beauty of Lucrezia's body that holds him prisoner.

Browning brings out clearly the timidity which Vasari' stressed as the central weakness in the character of Andrea. Like Hamlet, his fault is indecision and it is this part of the general moral weakness which makes him a failure. The words of Andrea could well be the echo of the poet's own yearning,

> "There burns a truer light of God in them,
>
> In their vexed, beating, stuffed and stopped-up-brain,
>
> Heart, or whate'er else, than goes on to prompt
>
> This low-pulse forthright craftsman's hand of mine.
>
> Their works drop groundwards, but themselves
>
> I know.
>
> Reach many a time a heaven that's shut to me
>
> Enter and take their place there sure enough,
>
> Though they come back and cannot tell the world.
>
> My works are nearer heaven, but I sit here."

(Lines 81-90)

The struggle between flesh and soul appears in all its intensity in "Fra Lippo Lippi". The Friar has been commissioned by a certain wealthy nobleman to paint pictures of saints. As he has been three weeks shut in his rooms, busy with his work, the lute-strings and songs of some passing girls lure him out. Brother Lippo had renounced the world when he had taken the oath, at the age of ten. But to him, life is beautiful with all it has to offer, and consequently he does not hesitate to renounce his priestly ordains for the satisfaction of mind, just as he had not hesitated to renounce the world for satisfaction of hunger. In this dramatic monologue, Browning has given a vivid pen-portrait of a friar, who can be identified with an exponent of the Renaissance Superbia. Considered from another viewpoint, Lippo appears to be a synonymous character of Browning himself, since he voices the opinions and aspirations of the latter. Whatever interpretation is given to the aforesaid monologue, nothing can detract from it's delightful zest for life, and for all things living. Lippo is comparable to a high priest of Nature, and he worships all the objects that are animate ________ even the most trivial "thing" in existence. The slightest sight or sound of nature causes him to vibrate with joy, and ecstatically sing the praise of the Maker.

The chief characteristic of the monologue that strikes us again and again is the deep love and respect the speaker has for all things living. Nothing is mean or lowly in the gamut of the universe ______ the emotion that fills his heart while looking out upon the starry night is in no way different from the sense of fulfillment he gets when he meets the night-revelers and comes "up with the fun." Fra Lippo sings the song of life, yet the sublimity does not become an obsession, or an emotion of frozen purity. For him life is as full of variety as of color, and gratification of the senses is as essential as that of the soul. The tone of the poem is a quaint, bantering one. Fra Lippo is not a serious overtly man; he is giving the guards an explanation of his action. Yet we feel this superficial frivolity hides and deeper emotion, made richer by Lippo's early experiences. As a boy, Lippo experienced the pangs of hunger _______ and strangely enough he joined the Church to satisfy this physical need. Having roamed about the streets with an empty stomach, young Lippo has realized the cost of life, and also the innate beauty and variety it holds. His words are therefore, not idle philosophical statements, Fra Lippo has lived a life, in the sense that he has experienced pain and pleasure and his senses have become sharpened and more responsive. Therefore, when he speaks of the difference between flesh and soul (life vs church) and also of the affinity between the two, he knows what he is talking about.

Browning presents his characters with devastating frankness, and the priest's admission could well be considered a blasphemy by the church authorities, yet he is not out to impress the officer by uttering untruths. Browning believed that the ultimate good matters ______ not the means employed to attain that "good". To assuage his physical want, Lippo once renounced the world of material pleasure, now he is as eager to renounce the world of the cloister to satisfy the senses. For him, life is a brief interlude, and a fulfillment of this life depends on how intensely a person has lived it. Lippo is a disciple of life and a believer of his own actions. The quaint strains of songs that occur and recurs as the narrative proceeds, helps to lighten the atmosphere and introduce a note of irrepressible buoyancy that the cold and pallid walls of the cloister have failed to subjugate. Thus, although Fra Lippo Lippi has failed in the eyes of his church brothers, he has understood the meaning of life.

The principal source is Vasari's "Life of Fra Lippo Lippi". Lippo has no inhibitions, and "flesh" is one of the key words in his monologue. His passion for female beauty is only one manifestation of the fascinated delight that he takes in the human scene". .... "Fra Lippo is a vivacious man with an imagination that is by no means confined to the world of the senses. The effect of the (animal) images he uses are by no means to make him appear a mere 'beast', but rather to emphasize his delight in the natural world, with which he has a deep instinctive sympathy."[16]

Painting, after religion, and history, is the great theme and subject matter of Browning's poetry. In *Fra Lippo Lippi,* he fused painting, history and religion. Fra Lippo's robust and vital individuality chafes against a variety of circumstances _____ by which he is caught: a childhood of poverty, the hypocritical asceticism of the Church, a sterile and stylized tradition in painting, the burgher patronage of the Medici. But the licentious painter - monk's energy and humanity, like that of the Renaissance in which he lives, are finally irrepressible.

---

[16]   "Browning's Major Poetry": Ian Jack. Ch. xii.

Many of Browning's monologues are exercises in self-justification, ________ not Browning justifying himself, but his characters justifying to their listeners a certain course of action, a set of beliefs, even their entire life." Fra Lippo has moved a long way from merely excusing himself for his midnight escapades among the ladies: his anger and frustration, warmed by the memories of his childhood and his life in the Carmine cloister, force him to articulate what he himself is, his love of the physical world, the nature and function of his realistic art. His sexuality is not just a lovable weakness in a licentious monk, but his itself a profoundly religious attitude towards the beauty of God's world:"[17]

> ". . . . you've seen the world
>
> The beauty and the wonder and the power,
>
> The shapes of things, their colours, lights and
>
> and shades.

---

[17]   "Robert Browning: Routledge Author Guides"

Changes and surprises, ____ and God made all!"

De Vane rightly emphasizes the relationship of Fra Lippo to his creator Browning. He (Browning) "could not have chosen a better poem with which to challenge the orthodox conception of poetry in the mid-nineteenth century, or one that better expresses the new elements in poetry that Browning was to introduce. Browning found in the Renaissance painter a very sympathetic character, like himself highly individualistic, suffering from the tyranny of artistic convention, and like himself energetic and instinct with seemingly well thought out aesthetic and religious opinions which claimed Browning's own."[18]

A subtle difference and at the same time, a similarity can be traced between Andrea and the painter monk, Fra Lippo. The latter is full of life, boisterous energy and is totally amoral.

---

[18] "A Browning Handbook" ___ Clyde De Vane. Pg. 219.

There is an excess of movement and color that forms a panoramic background against which, Fra Lippo's thoughts are presented. Andrea, on the contrary, is resigned, languid, immobile _____ apathetic. This is conveyed brilliantly to the readers by the slow-moving verse of his monologue. Lippi is free and unconventional; Andrea spends his lonely hours, by the window, and watches his wife going out to join her lover in the street. "The one painter is sociable and Chaucerian: the other is solitary. The one painter talks of what he will do, scurrying off at the end after promising to paint a fine new picture; the other talks of what he has done, and even more of what he might have done _______ or might he?"[19]

Whereas the ranging amorousness of Lippi leaves him free, luxuriousness had reduced Andrea to the condition of a slave. The very 'perfection' of his art *is a sign of his limitations*, and of his ultimate failure. One is reminded of two passages in

---

[19]   "The Men and Women Poems" - Ian Jack, Ch. XII.

Ruskin. The first occurs in Modern Painters; here he states that "in order to receive a sensation of power, we must see it in operation. Its victory, therefore, must not be achieved, but achieved, and therefore, imperfect. "The second theory is presented in *The Stones of Venice.* Here Huskia claims that two "great truths... belonging to the whole race" are "the confession of Imperfection, and the confession of Desire of Chance."

"The contrast between the two painters is drawn at a point beyond the common places of conventional morality: it might be argued that Andrea is faithful to an undeserving wife, while Lippi is clearly incapable of fidelity to any woman. It is much more important that Fra Lippo is faithful to the requirements of his art, while Andrea is not. The parable of the talents, which was never far from Browning's mind, is highly relevant to the two poems."[20]

---

[20]   "The Men and Women Poems" - Ian Jack, Ch. XII.

"The Bishop Orders his Tomb" is a vibrant monologue by a Bishop, who, having seemingly renounced 'worldly pleasure', is still an epicurean at heart. To interpret this monologue as a satire is to be blind to the subtlety of the poem. Browning was always interested in the vision of life that presented itself to a dying man: 'Sordelle', 'Prospice', 'Paracelsus'. Yet our expectation of a religious homily is mocked by every line of the Bishop's monologue, as his mind drifts from his nephews around him, to the mistress who had been their mother ______ and to 'Old Gandolf', whose jealousy had added piquancy to the Bishop's delight at possessing so beautiful a mistress. The revelation of immorality and hypocrisy should shock the reader, but the objective method of dealing with the subject ______ lessens the shock. We are persuaded to study the situation from the bishop's point of view. According to Browning, all truth is a matter of perspective, and it (truth) is related to events in the same way as point of view is related to landscape.

Instead of caring for the salvation of his soul, the bishop is concerned only with the destination of his body. 'His greatest fear has nothing to do with the judgment to come; it is simply the nightmare thought that the ingratitude of his illegitimate sons may lead them to economize in the construction of his tomb. As he conjures them to obey his wishes. . . . he does not rely on their sense of filial duty but solely on their expectation of material and fleshly rewards.'[21] Ruskin wrote in *Modern Painters* "I know no other piece of modern English, press or poetry, in which their is so much told, as in these lines, of the Renaissance spirit, its worldliness, inconsistency, pride, hypocrisy, ignorance of itself, love of art; of luxury, and of good Latin.[22]

On the death-bed of St. Praxed's Bishop, sensuality, greed, vanity, spite and the whole gamut of human frailties balance the

---

[21]   'Browning's Major Poetry: 'Ian Jack. Ch. XII, Pgs. 195-201.
[22]   'Modern Painters' Ruskin. Vol. IV, Ch. XX.

humanity of man against the responsibility and pretensions of priestly office. Browning's language was never so colourful than in the speech he gives the bishop on his death-bed; never did a character enjoy life in all its aspects with such intensity and pagan sensuality. The Bishop's enjoyment of life does not exclude anything. We find that the christian and pagan; divine and human; physical and intellectual beauty, are all fused in the intensity of the bishop's sensual imagination. Browning has presented before his readers the picture of a great humanist, a man both cultivated and culpable who, however, is inadequate as a bishop _____ but nevertheless luxuriates in the wonders, beauties and frailties of life. "The whole poem is riddled with contradictions and ironies, from the perfunctory blessings he bestows on his sons at the end. Two codes of conduct and morality could hardly have been more violently juxtaposed pg. 325-326. The Bishop, however, is quite without any sense of the contradictions and conflicts that are embodied in his monologue. Indeed, he is peculiarly single-minded in his pursuit of the good things of life, material, intellectual and spiritual. The conflict arises from the incongruity that so clearly exists between the man and his office."[23]

According to *A.R. Jones,* the bishop, is a product of the humanist tradition. Classically educated, he is a discriminating admirer of the arts and of beauty wherever found _____ in the world of nature, or in the nature of women, in the play of sunlight, or in the smell of incense. To the very end he continues to live in the world of the *senses:* 'so fair she was!' to quote Jones: "There is no doubt that by any reasonable standards of Christian morality the Bishop is a sinful man who betrayed his office and his church. There is, equally, no doubt that he justified his life by the sheer quality of his humanity, the pleasure he took in the experience of life itself. In fact he has

---

[23]   'Robert Browning and the Dramatic Monologue' A.R. Jones. Ch. XI, Pgs. 325 & 326.

lived as if his life were a work of art, created by himself, an artist of life whose art like the paintings of Fra Lippo is beyond the reach of morality."[24]

'*The Last Ride Together*' is one of the finest of Browning's dramatic monologues. In this poem, failure is glorified till the barb of pain gradually ceases to hurt. The speaker, rejected by the mistress, forgets his temporary sorrow in the contemplation of the happiness which awaits him in the afterlife, when he hopes to be reunited with his beloved. This dauntless faith prevents the speaker' tone from becoming agitated. The lover emphasizes success in the eye of God is preferable and superior to worldly success _____ and the reader feels that his (speaker) belief is shared by Browning. Unrequited love ceases to be painful, as the speaker realizes:

". . . . Still one must lead some life beyond,

— Have a bliss to die with, dim - descried . . ."

---

[24]   Ibid., pg. 326, Ch. XI.

and again:

"Earth being so good, would Heaven seem best?

Now Heaven and she are beyond this ride".

The Last Ride Together is one of Browning's supreme poems of *failure*. Here aspiration is not turned into achievement, but is forever frozen and intensified. Thus, 'The Last Ride Together' could be called an exceptional poem ___ that of success. According to *Ian Jack*:

"This is the utterance of a man who is in a sense obsessed by love, but this time the speaker might be described as a triumphant obsessive. The theme is Browning's favourite ____ that of striving the speaker has done all that he could, and the fact that he has not been successful is of less importance."[25]

The protagonist says in the monologue:

"Fail I alone in words and deeds?

___

[25]   'Browning's Major Poetry' Ian Jack. Pg. 161. Ch. XI.

Why, all men strive and who succeeds?"

The more fact of striving denotes a kind of success that makes life meaningful. The theme is different from the conventional lover's complaint. The poem is therefore, not one of failure but the reverse. Riding was often an important imaginative stimulus to Browning, and here it becomes a powerful imaginative symbol. It is implied that "among man's deepest wishes is that love might be enough _____ all sufficient and lasting: 'that such raptures are self-sufficient and enduring', as Browning phrased it."[26]

In yet another monologue of Browning, *'Abt Vogler'* the musician believes that the duty of mankind lies in composing beautiful hymns in praise of God. The artist might not be successful in the eyes of his worldly listener, but he has his reward:

---

[26]   "A Reader's Guide To Robert Browning." Norton. B. Crowell. Pg. 189.

"The high that proved too high, the heroic for earth

too hard.

The passion that left the ground to lose itself in the

sky,

Are music sent up to God by the lover and the bard;

Enough that he heard it once; we shall hear it by and

by."

Abt Vogler is conscious of the vision of evil, but believes implicitly that eventually good shall triumph. This faith makes him retain his equilibrium, and prevents a sense of insecurity. Truth is related to events as point of view is related to landscape. It is thus possible to arrive at a unity or totality of vision by confronting truth in all its aspects, be they ugly or beautiful. Thus:

"There shall never be one lost good! What was,

shall live as before;

The evil is null, is naught, is silence implying sound

What was good, shall be good, with, for evil, so

much good more;

On the earth the broken arcs; in the heaven, a perfect

round."

(Lines 69 -72)

Before concluding, it would be worthwhile to discuss two monologues — noted for their vibrant quality, and the underlying vision of evil: they are 'Childe Roland to the Dark Tower Came', and 'Caliban Upon Setebos'. No other poem has been interpreted so variously as 'Childe Roland . . .' Little is known about the origin of the poem. It is uncertain whether it was written in 1852, or during the following year. Browning's own statements are "it came to me as a kind of dream." He told Mrs. Orr - "my own marsh was made out of my head, ____ with some recollection of a strange solitary little tower I have come upon more than once in Massa-Carrara, in the midst of low hills."[27]

It is obvious that a number of visual details came together in his mind as he composed the poem, and *De Vane* is probably right in suggesting that the chapters in *'The Art of Painting'* by Gerard de Lairesse describing beauty and ugliness in landscape also influenced its composition. Yet the important question still remains: What did Browning make of his materials, and what does the poem mean? It is clear that the poem has a much greater psychological depth than the stories that helped to inspire it. In this monologue, the prisoners are all adventurers, yet they are not prisoners physically, ____ but have failed in a deeper, spiritual sense. The landscape in the other narratives are brief, uninteresting and entirely subservient to narrative and character, but here it has a psychological significance — 'the landscape is everything'.

---

[27]   'Robert Browning : New Letter' Pg. 172-173.

One can agree with De Vane in stating that the landscape in the poem is not an external thing merely. As we read the poem the terrifying and dreary territory that the Childe describes becomes slowly and gradually a *landscape of the mind,* as we move across (with the protagonist) the starved plain, with its sinister weeds, eerie atmosphere, old and macabre horse — in the last stages of starvation. He moves on, but he is always on feet. Childe Roland is a pilgrim, making his weary way along with no support except a stick or a sword to defend himself with. Images of waste, desolation and torture abound in the monologue. The word 'tophet's tool 'could well be a synonym for hell —— Tophet was "a place or object in the valley of Hinnom, . . . where human sacrifices were burned by idolatrous Israelites in the worship of Moloch. "Browning portrays the Childe not as a figure of despair, but a figure of valour. He is able to preserve his equilibrium even in the face of despair and horrible sights. There is a neglected social dimension in the symbolism. *D.V. Erdman* believes: that it should be read as "Browning's Industrial Nightmare"; *J. Kirkman* thinks it is an allegory of dying, or an archetype of rebirth—— the latter opinion is also shared by *C.R. Woodward.*

There is a passage in *'The Ancient Mariner'* by D.W. Harding which has an obvious relevance to Browning's poem: "The human experience around which Coleridge centers the poem is surely the depression and the sense of isolation and unworthiness which the Mariner describes in Part IV. The suffering he describes is of a kind which is perhaps not found except in slightly pathological conditions, ... He feels isolated . . . . . At the same time he is not just physically isolated but is socially abandoned. . . . All that is left, and especially, centrally, oneself, is disgustingly worthless. . . . With the sense of worthlessness there is also guilt. And enveloping the whole experience is the sense of sapped energy, oppressive weariness. . . ."28

A usual feature of such states of pathological misery is their apparent carelessness. The depression cannot be rationally explained; the conviction of guilt and worthlessness is out of "proportion to any ordinary offense actually committed."29

But the difference between the two poems (The Ancient Mariner vs Childe Roland) are at least as interesting as the similarities. Unlike the Mariner's, the Child's nightmare journey is a journey by land, Browning was not fascinated by the sea . . . and the Childe is a more active and striving figure than the Mariner. While it is clear that he is confronting a tremendous challenge, and that he refuses to give up, it is uncertain whether he feels guilty. Near the end, indeed, he certainly feels guilty, and blames himself for his unsuccess— he realizes that he has

---

28   D.W. Harding.
29   Scrutiny, 9 (March 1941).

failed to recognize the ultimate test, for which he has been preparing all his life:

> ". . . Dunce,
>
> Dotard, a-dozing at the very nonce,
>
> After a life spent training for the sight."

Our interpretation of the last line depends on our interpretation of the poem as a whole, or — to put the matter more accurately — our interpretation of the last line *grows out* of our interpretation of the poem as a whole. A number of critics have taken the final lines as a *record of failure*.

(i) R.J. Gratz - finds a connection with Bunyan, and states that the Child finds himself 'at last surrounded by the ugly heights of Doubting Castle, one more victim of Giant Despair.'

(ii) Betty Miller - Tells us that the vision which inspired the poem revealed to Browning 'in a landscape fully as ominous as that of Dante's *Inferno*. . . the the retribution appropriate to his own sin' — the failure to deliver the message to mankind.

(iii)   Mrs. Melchiori - considers that "Childe Roland's' turning off towards the dark tower is a form of suicide" resulting from despair occasioned by "the reversal and everturning of all the values which Browning accepted and in which he believed. Thus the poem is the triumph of evil and despair.[30]

The striking similarities between 'Childe Roland' and 'Prospice' has been pointed out by several critics. We recall that the seeaker in Prospice is so far from committing suicide that he wishes to approach 'the post of the fee' without fear and in full consciousness. The Childe, too, is successful, even if death is the condition of his success. The important question is— "What happens to the child after he blows the horn?" That is left to the

---

[30]   "Browning's Major Poetry; The Dramatic Romances of 1855", Ch. XI, Pg. 181.

imagination of the readers. Commenting on the concluding lines of the monologue, *Ian Jack* says: "That we do not know, and this is (no doubt) the point at which the dreamer awakes. Yet, whatever is about to happen, by blowing the horn the dreamer triumphs. Whether we are to suppose that he defeats the giant. . . or is killed by him, it is hard to believe that he is *other than successful,* even if death is the condition of his success."[31]

When, near the end of his life, Browning was asked whether he accepted one particular allegorical interpretation, he replied: "Oh, no, not at all. Understand, I don't repudiate it either. I only mean I was conscious of no allegorical intention in writing it. . . . (It) came to me as a kind of dream. . . . I did not know then what I meant beyond that, and I'm sure I don't know now. But I am very fond of it."[32]

---

[31]   "Browning's Major Poetry; The Dramatic Romances of 1855", Ch. XI, Pg. 183.
[32]   "The Browning's" — Lilian Whiting. Pg. 261.

To conclude, Childe Roland's dreamlike logic, like coleridge's "Kubla Khan", can accommodate a bewildering array of images drawn from Browning's reading — from *Jack and the Beanstalk* to Dante; from the allegory of Spenser to the brutal industrial landscape lying behind Elizabeth's "The Cry Of the Children."

In religious poetry, particularly the poems of 1855's Browning always fear and anxiety about the loss of a loving God by humorous realism and skilful casuistry. . . . Childe Roland shares a terrible contrast with contemporary documents like: Kierkegaard's "Fear & Trembling" and Carlyle's "Sartor Resartus."

"Childe Roland is Browning's contribution to an evolving portrait of a spiritual wasteland which found expression in Tennyson's "The Holy Grail" (1869), in Thomson's "The City of Dreadful Night" (1874), in Hardy's

"The Darkling Thrush" (1900) and which culminated in Eliot's "The Waste Land" (1922).[33]

The final monologue which I intend to discuss is *'Caliban Upon Setebos'*, subtitled 'Natural Theology in the Island'. This is an argument in a dramatic framework. It illustrates Browning's flair for the grotesque. . . . What makes 'Caliban. . .' unique is the imaginative power which renders it truly dramatic. *Theodore Parker*, the American Unitarian said: 'A man rude in spirit must have a rude conception of God. He thinks of the deity like himself. If a buffalo had a religion, his conception of deity would be probably a buffalo, fairer limbed, stronger and swifter than himself, grazing in the fairest meadow of heaven.'

Caliban's reasoning follows the same lines. He believes that Setebos, whom he conceives after his own image,

---

[33]   "Browning : Routledge Author Guides" Roy. E. Gridley, Ch. IV, Pg. 89.

lives in the moon being the creator of all sublunary things. He further believes that Setebos is morally different, like Hardy's President of the Immortals. Browning deftly portrays the mind of Caliban, semi—human, semi—beast. Since envy is one of Caliban's ruling features, he consequently attributes to Setabes an envious temperament. Despite his distorted sensibility, Caliban made a deep appeal to Browning's imagination, and the poet took great care to depict his character perfectly. The vitality of the poem is due to the fact that the figure of Caliban made a deep impression on Browning, who was obsessed with the theme of 'vision of evil'. He has also acknowledged to Elizabeth Barrett his curious interest in insects and other creeping things. Keats could identify himself with lowly and apparently ugly creatures. A beautiful description is found in his poem 'Sibrandus Schf Burgensis'. Browning presents Caliban as a comic creature, but he is not grotesque. As the monologue continues, we find that gradually Caliban develops from 'a mouthpiece of his creator' to an individual personality. Browning is here using his dramatic genius, to the best of his ability. He is giving rein to his delight in the grotesque, for a definite purpose. "He is satirizing on any purely natural theology, by giving us the reflections on the nature of God of a creature much inferior to man, yet supposedly man, yet supposedly man's ancestor.'[34]

Thus we see that through his life, Browning continued in his search for originality — both as subject matter, and also in the technique he adopted while writing his dramatic monologues. He was concerned in Men, not in mankind. His abiding faith in the essential goodness of man, and his saving grace of optimism, gave rise to the fore mentioned poems. Dishonest, morbid, evil his protagonists may be, but they all have a logical excuse to offer. Life is a mixture of good and evil — and Browning believed each is essential to the other. His

---

[34]   "Browning's Major Poetry— Dramatis Personae", Ian Jack, Ch. XIII.

vision of evil, is therefore, actually his ability to perceive life as

a whole — he is the eighteenth century realist.

***

Chapter II

An Analysis of Robert Browning's *'La Saisiaz'*

La Saisiaz published in 1878 (15 May) along with *The Two Poets of Croisic* deals with the theme of death and immortality. *La Saisiaz* has much in common with *Christmas-Eve and Easter-Day* **(1850),** for while the latter poem had been prompted by the death of Browning's mother; *La Saisiaz* was occasioned by the death of Miss Anne Smith, a close friend of the poet and his sister. Miss Smith had been staying with Browning and his sister near Mount Saleve, Geneva, and her untimely death was a profound shock to the poet. Worth mentioning is the fact that Miss Smith and Browning had been discussing the subject of death, the immortality of the soul, and the possibility of an after-life earlier in the week.

La Saisiaz is at once a meditation and a revaluation of the poet's personal difficulties in the matters of faith and doubt. The fact that the poet had planned to climb Mount Saleve with Anne Smith made her death on the morning of the proposed climb doubly difficult to accept and come to terms with. Her death became at once a personal loss and at the same time symbolic of the mystery of evil. The incident induced Browning to examine again the grounds whereon his faith rested.

La Saisiaz published in 1878 (15 May) along with ***The Two Poets of Croisic*** deals with the theme of death and immortality. ***La Saisiaz*** has much in common with ***Christmas-Eve and Easter-Day* (1850),** for while the latter poem had been prompted by the death of Browning's mother; *La Saisiaz* was occasioned by the death of Miss Anne Smith, a close friend of the poet and his sister. Miss Smith had been staying with Browning and his sister near Mount Saleve, Geneva, and her untimely death was a profound shock to the poet. Worth mentioning is the fact that Miss Smith and Browning had been discussing the subject of death, the immortality of the soul, and the possibility of an after-life earlier in the week. This discourse on 'the Soul and Future Life' had occupied their minds on the evening preceding the death of Miss Smith. Consequently with the tragedy, the subject suddenly lost its facade of objective and academic interest. The personal nature of the poet's grief and the urgency of the situation lead to a fresh review of the topic.

La Saisiaz is at once a meditation and a revaluation of the poet's personal difficulties in the matters of faith and doubt. The fact that the poet had planned to climb Mount Saleve with Anne Smith made her death on the morning of the proposed climb doubly difficult to accept and come to terms with. Her death became at once a personal loss and at the same time symbolic of the mystery of evil. The incident induced Browning to examine again the grounds whereon his faith rested. The poem is an articulate elaboration of the question that was foremost in Browning's mind as he struggled to grasp the fact that Miss Smith was dead:

Did the face, the form I lifted as it lay, reveal the loss

Not alone in life but soul?

(Lines 173-174)

La Saisiaz is presented without the usual cover of a dramatic disguise, and this frank revelation of self is at once appealing and convincing.

The poem is a meditation on the possibility of an after-life and the sense of personal grief causes the poet to view the topic with extraordinary clarity and depth. The debate within the poet's own spirit finds expression within the dramatic framework of the poem.

The opening section is replete with various images-the long, leisurely walks, the superb scenery, the restful, unexplored nooks and the scintillating yet human conversation between the poet, his sister, and Miss Smith present a charming picture. The life in the chalet seems an invigorating existence. Yet the apparent stability has something of the nature of an interlude. The death of Miss Smith breaks into the contented world and shocks the poet out of his prior equanimity. The description of the picturesque setting gradually passes into a long and subtle course of reasoning on the probability of a future life. The speaker's affirmation is eloquent, but he does this dogmatically and without self consciousness.

The monologue commences with the poet narrating the sights and sounds that greet him on his gradual ascent to the summit of Mount Saleve, yet, as the monologue proceeds, this apparent 'narrative' subtly changes shape and becomes a touching and sensible record of the poet's thoughts and arguments upon the subjects of life and death. The transmutation is so gradual, so balanced, that it does not hamper the style of the poem. The conversational tone in matched with

an effortless meter, making the final proclamation acceptable :

... he at least believed in the Soul, was very sure of God.

(line 604)

The gist of **La Saisiaz**, then, deals with the ephemerality of life

or should we call it the 'apparent' ephemerality?

The title of the poem is appropriate and serves to

emphasize Browning's love of paradox. It could be interpreted

in diverse ways. It could well be that Browning chose to name

his monologue after the chalet where he had spent those

pleasant hours in the company of Anne Smith. It could also be

that by naming his effort **'La Saisiaz'** (the Sun) Browning

wishes to draw the attention of his readers to the affirmation that

there is a life hereafter. The 'sun' symbol has been repeatedly

used in the past to signify 'source of light and energy', 'life', and

'immortality'. The connotations affixed to the word in the past had not become obsolete with the passing of years. Considered against the backdrop of the nineteenth century, *La Saisiaz* may well stand for the Sun, and stretching the concept even further, 'immortality'. Whatever the primary thoughts of Browning may have been, the title is justified.

Browning starts the poem by assuming the existence of God, and the immortal quality of the soul. These are facts which are at once accepted as (1) certain, and (2) incapable of being proved. Since Browning wishes to rest his argument solely on what *he* knows to be a certain fact, he wishes to speak only for himself and avoids charting out a philosophy for other people. There are two things that the speaker knows for certain--his own existence, and that of a 'non'-self' existing independently from him:

> I have questions and am answered. Question,
>
> answer presupposes.
>
> Two points: that the things itself which questions,

answers, *is*, it knows'.

As it also knows the thing perceived outside itself, a force

Actual ere its own beginning, operating through its course,

Unaffected by its end that this thing likewise needs must

be;

Call this--God, then, call that--soul, and both--the only

facts for me.

Prove them facts" that they ***o'erpass my power of proving,***

proves them such:

Fact it is I know I know not something which is fact as

much.

(lines 217-224)

The aim of the speaker is to arrive at a faith regarding the

immortality of the soul, and this movement is intended to pivot

on a consideration of the two unprovable yet known

entities--soul and God. Browning rules out the possibility that

the doubts that trouble the human heart can be set at rest by

Christina revelation *alone*. Yet the subject of Christian revelation is neither derided nor by-passed. The poem is an attempt of Browning to find an answer in human terms to the questions that have occupied man's mind from time immemorial :

> Life thus owned unhappy, is there supplemental happiness
> Possible and probable in life to come? or must we count
> Life a curse and not a blessing, summed-up its whole amount;
> Help and hindrance, joy and sorrow? (lines 204-207)

Having weighed the pros and cons of such an examination into the paradoxical nature of life, the speaker resolves to continue in his quest:

> Why should I want courage here?
> I will ask and have an answer, with no favor, with no

fear,

From myself. How much, how little, do inwardly believe

True that a controversial doctrine? (Lines 207-210)

The quest of the speaker is balanced upon the fact that although 'I am' is the starting point of all knowledge to man, the resulting discovery is 'I myself am what I know rot'. For each man, his individual experience of pain and pleasure, doubt and hope remains the essential reality-- 'this is sure, the rest surmise'. Consequently, for each individual, knowledge rests on the fact of his own experience and existence. This idea is developed further along the monologue, in the lines 561-571.

There are two lines of reasoning within the consciousness of the speaker. An existence teeming with sorrow and evil can be accepted only by a faith in a second life. The first part of the poem (1-140) is a vivid description of the surrounding landscape. The painstaking attention to detail makes the reader aware of the poet's descriptive ability and of his equally strong impulse to immortalize the place where Anne Egerton Smith lies buried. Yet the colorful pageant is brought to rest with:

> . . . there's something more than Nature, man requires,
>
> And that, useful as is Nature to attract the tourist's foot,
>
> . . . the spirit also needs a comfort reached
>
> By no help from a lake or mountain . . .(lines 100-104)

The second movement of **La Saisiaz** (lines 140-216) deals with the possibility of life after death, and with the moral implications of the conclusion that the speaker hopes to reach. The poem's meaning evolves as an elaboration of the question 'Does the soul survive the body?/Is there God's self, no or yes?' The evidence of this world does not point to 'a cause all-good, all-wise, all-potent'. Since a disbelief in a life after death only leads us to an impasse, it is worthwhile to change position and examine the argument from a fresh perspective, namely, can the sufferings of this world be endured if man has hope of personal immortality?

The lines that bring the second movement of the first section to a close are at once tender and resonant with faith. The poet's abiding love for his wife acts as a lodestar, infusing him with the hope that 'from this life I pass into a better, there/where that lady lives of whom enamored was my soul.

It is worth nothing that throughout the monologue the tussle is revealed in the mind and heart of the speaker. The reiteration of the words 'I', 'my', 'mine' serves to show that at no point does the speaker claim objective validity for the conclusions he arrives at. The fruit of his *own* experience and his *own* perception emerges as the premise of the theological argument :

Well, and wherefore shall it daunt *me*, when 'tis *I myself* am tasked,

When, by weakness, weakness questioned, weakly

answers-- weakly asked?

. . . whispered by *my soul* to *me*. . . .

I shall no more dare to mimic such response in futile

speech,

Pass off human lisp as echo of the sphere-song out of reach.

(lines 147-154)

And again later on in the argument :

> *I myself* am what I know not . . .
>
> What to *me* is pain and pleasure: this is sure, the rest--
>
> surmise. . . .
>
> If (to *my own sense, remember*! though none other feel
>
> the same!)   (lines 260-268)

Understandably, the conclusion of the debate between Fancy
and Reason is not asserted as being generally true, but offered
tentatively as the speaker's own reasoning. The scheme of

values that evolve with the progress of the monologue are based

on the speaker's own experience (lines 287-292).

La Saisiaz has been set down as 'a moan out of

temporary depression' by H.C. Duffin, and the lines that have

received strongest disapproval are the ones mentioned above. A

careful reading of the poem dispels this allegation. The single

subjunctive 'if' provides the key to the discord and the meaning

of the sequential sentence hinges upon this word. The lines that

have been often quoted to suggest the pessimistic quality of the

poem are as follows :

> I must say--or choke in silence-- 'However came my fate,
>
> Sorrow did and joy did nowise, life well weighed,
>
> preponderate.' (Lines 332-333)

It is true that once torn from the context, and presented without

the prefix 'if', the lines appear to be almost unique in their

pessimism. But such a method defeats the purpose of the poem, for the lines have to be considered within the framework of the monologue and not accepted as a 'segment' of the poet's message. When A.C. Pigou and W.C. DeVane (among other critics) regret the 'pusillanimous' and 'doubtful' tone of *La Saisiaz,* they are making the same mistake that has caused the lines from **Pippa Passes** to be wrenched from the actual body of the poem and made to appear to cornerstone of a 'glib' philosophy.

The purpose of the subjunctive 'if' is to imply conditions contrary to the chartered facts, thus :

If the harsh throes of the prelude die not off into the
swell
Of that perfect piece they sting me to become a-strain
for, *if*
Roughness of the long rock-chamber lead *not* to the last
of cliff,
. . . *if* this life's conception, new life fails to realise . . .

(Them) I must say or choke in silence . . .

(lines 322-333)

Clearly what Browning is trying to say here is that if the adverse condition had been irrevocably true, *if* the 'harsh throes of the prelude' continued *without* the final 'swell', *then,* and only *then* would his life be marked by sorrow and not with joy. The sentiment that informs the aforementioned lines finds a companion source in ***The_Guardian Angel.*** Here, again, it is easy to disregard the subjunctive and pronounce the poem as evidence of Browning's denial of evil.

The following lines from ***The Guardian Angel*** are a striking parallel in their syntactical structure, (if not in their subject-matter) to ***La Saisiaz*** :

If ever this was granted, I would rest

My head beneath thine . . .

And all lay quiet, happy and suppressed.

How soon all worldly wrongs would be repaired!

I think about how I should view the earth and skies.

And sea, when once again my brow was bared

After thy healing, with such different eyes.

(lines 22-32, iv, v)

By the use of subjunctive, Browning is admitting the existence of evil, just as he had implied the contrary fact (existence of good) in **La Saisiaz.** In both the poems the emphasis is on the transient nature of evil, and **not** upon its illusory nature. Life is not all-good, but neither is it unrelieved suffering, and under no circumstances is evil unreal or 'suffer for transmuting'.

The central section of **La Saisiaz** (lines 217-404) involves the speaker reminiscing upon his own experience. He is forced to acknowledge that life can offer no meaning or coherence unless it be viewed as probationary:

> . . . there is no reconciling wisdom with a world
> distraught,

Goodness with triumphant evil, power with failure in the aim . . .

If you bar me from assuming earth to be a pupil's place,

And life, time, with all their chances, changes, just probation-space,

Mine for me. (lines 266-271)

Again and again the poet emphasizes that all his reasoning is based on his personal experience 'knowledge stands on my experience ...' It is essential for every individual to discover the truth for himself, in proportion to the capacity of reasoning afforded to him.

Worth comparing are lines 274-278 from *La Saisiaz* and those (13-16, 27-29) from *Christmas-Eve*. While Browning stressed the validity of personal choice and experience in the absence of concrete, external proof, he is by no means guilty of implying that truth is relative. Truth is absolute, but the imperfections of man permit him to reach at best an approximation of this 'absolute truth'. Man's conviction should find a basis in his personal experience.

Turning to judge the world according to the nature of his own experience (lines 293-348) the speaker discovers innumerable paradoxes.

Turning to judge the world according to the nature of his own experience (lines 293-348) the speaker discovers innumerable paradoxes. To a casual reader the God of *La Saisiaz* does not seem to offer any additional promise or comfort and provides a curious parallel to the callous indifference of Caliban's imagined deity.

The speaker rejects the assumption that only by experiencing the pangs of pain and suffering can happiness be apprehended more completely. The following lines are a direct rebuttal of the idea that Browning refuted the existence of evil

in *La Saisiaz* :

> What, no way but this that man may learn and lay to
>
> heart how rife
>
> Life were with delights would only death allow their
>
> taste of life?
>
> Must the rose sigh 'Pluck--I perish!' must the eve weep
>
> 'Gaze--I fade!' . . .
>
> Can we love but on condition that the thing we love
>
> must die?
>
> Needs there groan a world in anguish just to teach us
>
> sympathy--
>
> Multitudinously wretched that we, wretched too, may
>
> guess
>
> What is a preferable state of universal happiness?
>
> (lines 307-314)

Working on the previous theory, until and unless the lesson man learns on earth is to be put to use elsewhere, somewhere beyond the finite limits of this life, the present pain and suffering would be devoid of meaning :

> Nay, were fancy fact, were earth and all it holds illusion
> mere,
> Only a machine for teaching love and hate and hope and
> fear
> To myself the sole existence, single truth 'mid falsehood--
> well!
> If the harsh throes of the prelude die not off into the
> well . . .
> I must say or choke in silence . . . preponderate.

(lines 319-334)

There is an element of hope in the poet's reasoning that an omnipotent God could not have created this world without the blessing of an after-life. The seemingly limited and imperfect qualities of God (line 348) are put aside, while the speaker determines to reach 'truth's self' from examining the basic premises. These are (1) the existence of God, and (2) the existence of the soul. The third conviction to be arrived at is the hope of personal immortality, and the second part of the poem sees the unfolding of this problem. To examine the problem, Browning introduces the dialogue form. The debate between Fancy and Reason progresses as a development of the principles laid down in the first part of the poem, while 'soul' takes the position of the umpire, thus:

> God is, and the soul is, and, a certain, after death shall be.
>
> Put this third to use in life, the time for using facts! (lines 408-409)

Before moving on to the second part of the poem (lines 405-545) it will be well to consider the lines where the speaker suggests that the anomalies of the world can be resolved (in theory, if not in practice) on the assumption that there is a life to come :

> . . . Only grant a second life; I acquiesce
>
> In this present life as failure, count misfortune's worst assaults
>
> Triumph, not defeat, assured that loss so much the more exalts
>
> Gain about to be. (lines 358-361)

This boon of a second life granted, reconciliation would be possible:

> Worst were best, defeat were triumph, utter loss were utmost gain
>
> Can it be, and must, and will it? (lines 389-390)

Like the speaker of ***Prospice*** it should be possible to say:

> For sudden the worst turns the best to the brave,
>
> The black minute's at end,

And the element's rage, the fiend-voices that rave,

Shall dwindle, shall blend,

Shall change, shall become first a peace out of pain,

Then a light ... (lines 21-26)

The second part of the poem explores this possibility of a future life and presents the issue in the form of a dialogue between Fancy and Reason. Fancy starts with the assumption 'that after the body dies the soul lives again'. To the two facts 'acknowledged late' a third and equally pertinent one is added-- 'God *is,* and the soul *is*, and as certain, after death shall *be*.'

Line 408 is immediately followed by a more dynamic advice--' Put this third to use in life, the time for using facts!' Since the purpose of life is action, it is important to have a clear picture of the meaning and significance of life before an action can be accomplished. Since human knowledge is imperfect, the 'surmises' or 'postulates' that go beyond the facts help to sustain the picture of a perfect and purposeful universe and an

All-Benevolent God. Considered from this point, the 'postulates' cease to be mere 'fancy' and merge into 'facts', or to put the matter in simpler terms, the postulates once accepted as 'facts' make human life intelligible.

Discussing the relationship of 'facts' and 'postulates' F.E. L. Pristley writes in his essay:

> Our knowledge being limited, we must supplement it, or indeed arrange its fragments, with the help of postulates which 'go beyond the facts'. Since these postulates are a vital part of the system of relations which turns 'facts' into 'knowledge', they can be properly considered themselves 'facts' in the popular sense (which equates facts with knowledge).

In **La Saisiaz** 'fancy' does not mean poetic imagination but the popular significance of the word, namely 'fiction'.

The dialogue that follows is at once a debate, and a mutual effort of Reason and Fancy to search for truth. Reason joins in with Fancy in attempting to elicit how one should act in this life if he had the assurance of a future state of existence. Although Fancy and Reason agree in the main, namely, that it should be known to all men that the present life is a probation period, Reason rightly points out that such a knowledge would destroy the efficacy of action involving choice. Once the postulate becomes a certainty, man's moral nature would automatically lose credit. Secondly, granted that there is a future life, a better existence, the immediate query is why then should man delay in obtaining entry to this life-to-come? The promise of a happier state can rightly tempt man to put an end to his life, and to the burden attached to it. How far can such an action be condoned?

Bibliography

1. Robert Browning's Poetry, Norton Critical Edition. London: 1979

2. 'A Reading of La Saisiaz', from Robert Browning: A Collection of Critical Essays, F.E.L. Pristly: Routledge: 1966

3. The Poetry of Browning: A Critical Introduction Philip Drew. OUP, London: 1972

4. A Critical History of English Literature : David Daiches, Vol I and II. Supernova Publishers, New Delhi: 2019

5. Philip Drew: The Poetry of Browning. Methuen: London: 1970

6. Hugh Walker: The Greater Victorian Poets. S. Sonnenschein and Company: New York, 1895

7. C.L.Ryals: Browning's Later Poetry. Cornell University Press, New York, 1975

8. W.C. De Vane: A Browning Handbook. Appleton – Century Crofts, New York, 1955

9. A.Symons: An Introduction to the Study of Browning. Cassell & Company, Limited, London: Paris & New York, 1886

10. G.K.Chesterton: Robert Browning, Macmillan & Co.,Limited: London, 1903

11. F.L.Lucas: Ten Victorian Poets,Cambridge at the University Press: London, 1948

12. Alexander: An Introduction to Browning, Ginn and Company: Boston , USA, 1889

13. Legouis and Cazamian: A History of English Literature. J.M. Dent & Sons Ltd: London, 1964

14. Sir Humphrey Milford: Robert Browning : Poetry and Prose. Oxford University Press: London, 1943

15. Compton and Rickett: A History of English Literature. T.C & E.C. Jack; London, 1912

16. Mary Wilson: A Primer of Browning. Nabu Press: Berlin, 2010

17. A. Sharp: Victorian Poets. Cornell University Library's Print: New York, 1891

18. C.H. Herford: Browning. Wentworth Press: London, 2016

19. W.T.Young: Browning :Selected Poems. OUP: London, 1929